DREAMS & SCHEMES

DREAMS & SCHEMES

Love and Marriage in Modern Times

Abigail Heyman

PICTURE PROJECT | NEW YORK

The participation of brides and grooms, their families and guests is in the heart of this book. They have invited me, and thus you, into some of the most intimate moments of their lives, and shared with us their joy and their pain. I thank them.

The often uncertain task of expressing a personal view of the world begs for unflinching critical support. Friends and colleagues have generously given me that, especially Lynn Bernstein, Jonathan Bloch, Ethan Hoffman, Jeff Jacobson, and Alain Jullien. Archive Pictures has sustained this project with the flexibility and breadth of its belief in documentary photography.

And finally, I want to thank the two people in my personal life who keep the energy flowing: Donald Bloch and Lazar Heyman-Bloch. They not only belong first on the list of supportive critics, but also—in their daily love— have made most of it fun.

Grateful acknowledgment is made for permission to reprint the lyrics on page thirty-seven, by Richard Wilbur from the show *Candide*, music by Leonard Bernstein.

Library of Congress Catalog Card number: 86-72917
ISBN 0- 9632551-2-6 (cloth)
ISBN 0- 9632551-3-4 (paper)
Printed in England by
Balding + Mansell International Limited

PICTURE PROJECT, Inc. is a non–profit organization that increases the public's access to photography of commitment, depth, and visual courage. For more information about our books and other projects, contact Picture Project at 40 West 12th Street, NY, NY 10011, fax: (212) 727-1126, tel: (212) 255-8815.

For Donald

"I read for pleasure, mark you. In general I like wedding bells at the end of novels. 'They married and lived happily ever after'—why not? it has been done." *A. Edward Newton*

Here is a feast of weddings, from the point of view of an enchanted spectator and participant. Here is the tension and the celebration, the romance and the reality, the humor and the toughness of those who participate in life's most intense and complex ritual. I respect these people. More than that—at every wedding I attend, I am in awe. The human spirit, in all its frailty and strength, is here.

I say "wedding" and a stereotype immediately comes to mind: the country church, the virgin bride, the bride's doting parents, the smiling-tense groom's parents, the proud best man, the hopeful maid of honor, the silver embossed napkins, "Harvey and Hannah" on the swizzle sticks—it is printed, public, permanent.

But I go to a wedding, and it isn't a stereotype at all: it is a two-minute ceremony at City Hall, or an overnight camping trip in the woods. Two of the bride's former lovers are there; or I meet the groom's six-year-old daughter. A bride's parents are divorced, and her father isn't there to "give her away" because her mother wouldn't come if he did. Or, a groom's parents are sour because they don't approve of a bride who won't change her name. Or, our modern Harvey and Hannah have both been married before, and we know as they take their vows—"till death do us part"—they believe them, and they also believe that divorce is the better alternative to a bad marriage.

At its most powerful, the wedding radically changes lives. At its least, it marks those changes. From King Edward giving up his throne for Wallace Simpson 50 years ago, to Superman becoming a mortal man to marry Lois Lane a few summers ago, the wedding is the watershed, the Great Divide.

Whether brides and grooms are passionately in love, or painfully compromised, they are truly stars for the day. Children are brushed and scrubbed to look their best—the photographer will make it permanent. The bride's mother, who herself had an expedient wartime wedding, now finally gets the chance to make a wedding the way she really wanted it. Sensing the truth that equals marry equals, parents see their total life work as parents evaluated. Siblings who have lived together intimately all their lives, now become occasional visitors in each others' homes—or even cities. The children/stepchildren also become wedded, for better or for worse, though it is extremely rare for the ceremony to acknowledge that. Guests look for mates of their own, or renew their own vows, or perhaps, regret them. There is no event in our lives as emotionally charged and varied as a wedding.

In the making of this book, my role as a photographer is, at best, peculiar. At hundreds of weddings, I have only twice been the official photographer. I am, instead, part guest, part photographer, part friend, part confidant, part consultant, and in large part ignored. I have, on one occasion, been seated at the head table, and on another, been asked not to talk to the guests. And everything in between. Though coming as a journalistic photographer, I usually bring a small gift. I don't know why—it just feels like the right thing to do. And it confuses people's expectations of me. That's useful.

When photographing, I try to arrive while everyone is busy with the preparations. I am frequently the only one around for the nervous bride or groom to talk to. And perhaps having no continuing relationship with them, I become a safe deposit place for the stories and feelings that otherwise might never be told.

Some photographers feel the camera separates them from their own feelings about people and events. To the contrary, the camera makes me closer. I could go to any one of these weddings without a camera, and—unless I was a member of the couple's most intimate circle—I would never notice their reasons for marrying, their expressions of feelings, their intimate stories, their dreams, or their schemes. I would chitchat with the other guests, drink champagne, dance, offer my sincere best wishes and best hopes. But with a camera, I notice.

I used to believe that crying at weddings was a silly ritual for the sentimental who indulged themselves. Now that I have seen, as a "cool, objective observer/journalist," what really goes on at weddings, I always cry. They are invariably sentimental and emotionally charged events. The camera, far from making me a detached observer, has confronted me with the human drama of the wedding and, indeed, of life itself.

I also photograph weddings because there was something in my own weddings that remained unresolved. Going to other people's weddings with a camera has put me in touch with my personal drama, too.

People have asked me, when they heard I was working on a book about marriage, "Are you pro or con?" The question took me by surprise. The meaning of marriage seems far more complicated than that.

More to the point, people have asked me, "Why is an ardent feminist like you married?" or "Is your feminism a mere matter of equal pay for equal work under the law, or didn't you have something deeper on your mind about power between women and men?"

In the recent past, some feminists—in disapproving of the power relationships that had existed between men and women—disapproved of men, or of any intimate relationship between men and women, and certainly of marriage. Most women found that those thoughts left them in an untenable relationship to the world. And they came to think of themselves as less radical.

I believe that easy answers to that, in fact, accept the status quo. To believe that there is no equality possible in a male-female relationship, and to refuse to intimately relate to men because one accepts that the male will win the more controlling position, means to buy in to the prevailing ideology. For myself, it has always seemed far more radical to try to work out those power problems on the front lines—on a daily and very personal basis. But that is not the calm and peaceful dream of marriage that I had before the feminist revolution.

I'd like to say that in my present marriage, we only fight about sex and money. It's not true. We also fight about child care, household responsibilities, space, and time. And beneath many of these issues is the basic fighting issue—power. Of course, power in each other's lives is also the sure sign that the relationship is meaningful to us.

I have been married twice. The first time I was infatuated with a man with whom I wanted to have an affair. It was too early for me to make any commitments about the rest of my life, but my parents were both getting anxious. My having that affair frightened my father, who firmly believed—at least in front of me—that women should be virgins when they married, and that once I had been seduced, I was unmarriageable, save perhaps to the man who had done the damage. (Big issue over little tissue, indeed!)

It was also true that my parents' anxiety was my own, for it was a time and place where women who never married were thought to lead wasted and unbearably unhappy lives. The marriage proposed to me seemed a viable possibility—especially since I had no assurance of what my other options in life would be. I believe it was with my best interests at heart, in the light of what we then knew, that my family and I all supported this first marriage.

Meanwhile, I was half expecting my fiancé to call it off. During the engagement, my mother planned a gorgeous home wedding, complete with flowers, photographers, the descent down a grand staircase, and guests I hardly knew. While all this proceeded, I kept consulting Emily Post and Amy Vanderbilt for advice on how to cancel a wedding at the last moment, but neither had a word to say on the subject. Wedding gifts kept rolling in, I kept waiting for him to cancel, he never did.

The machinery, once set in motion, has a momentum of its own. It's very hard to get out of it at that point. Strangely, it's easier to think of going through with it and busting up later. My first marriage ended in a divorce.

At most weddings today, there is some allusion to the prospect of divorce, a sword hanging over the whole event, a sorrowful reminder that things may not work out as planned. Most people are shocked at how high the divorce rate is. Quite the opposite, knowing how difficult it is for people to make a lifetime commitment, to accommodate another person, to work out the power struggles of marriage in a way they can happily live with, I sometimes think it is remarkable how many marriages stay intact.

When we decided to have a child, my lover and I committed ourselves to live together permanently. At the time, I was very clear about wanting *not* to "marry". It seemed then, that marriage—for women—meant having all of the responsibility and none of the power. And I didn't want others to treat me as someone's wife, to expect that decisions were not my own anymore, or to think of me as less alert and less capable than they had before.

Two years later, circumstances had changed and we needed the legal protections the government would give us in a marriage. My second wedding was a secret from my original family, many of whom didn't approve. Nor was it a joyous event, at that time, for my husband's children, who hadn't wanted a stepmother, with all that that implies. The ceremony celebrated our allegiance to each other, and it is hard to celebrate with others who are pained by the same event.

We were married at City Hall with four close friends and our baby in attendance. At home afterwards, our small group shared champagne and good feelings. There was a preference for intimacy over pomp and circumstance. It made me understand that the intensity of celebration at a wedding is not related to the arrangements.

I got married for the money. Marriage is, after all, a business contract. Hardly anyone ever mentions that, but most people are aware of it at some level. People rarely know what the contract says before they sign on. Furthermore, the legislature can rewrite the agreement without our approval. Few pay attention.

But I do not believe the reasons for my wedding were as simple as money and legal protections. I know more was going on. The meaning of the event continues to reveal itself to me in more and more complex ways. So when I go to photograph weddings, before the ceremony starts, I ask the modern couple, "Why are you getting married?"

"So I can answer the phone on Sunday mornings."

"Why not?"

"It just feels right."

"I never thought anyone would want to marry me."

"It'll make my children more comfortable."

"It'll make my parents more comfortable."

"I want him to be family."

"It makes something solid."

Everybody has a secret, a hidden plan for what is really going to be. Therein lies the concealment, the hypocrisy, the power manipulation. She is going to change him; he's going to use her—they have schemes, not just dreams. And yet, they are hoping against hope that they can do it in a way that can preserve their love and their joy in each other.

I've schemed in my life. And I can't talk about that. Frankly, I tried to write more about my weddings. I find it embarrassing. There are so many private secrets involved. There are the ghosts, the concerns about being offensive or unfair, the not wanting to own up to things that now seem alien. And also, perhaps, because I didn't know then what the secret plan was, what the scheme was. I was only dealing with the dream and I didn't know what it meant.

On some level, schemes are more honest than dreams, and just as legitimate. The schemes are about negotiating a relationship with a family of origin: I married an older brother because I wanted a caring older brother to make up for the antagonism between my original older brother and myself. The schemes are about your economic stake in what's going on: You're arranging for material comfort and security in a cold and forbidding world. The schemes are about your private agenda: You need a companion for hard times.

In the tradition of romantic love, schemes are regarded as ignoble, trashy motives. But they are not trash, they are a big piece of what we are all about. What's so terrible about trying to resolve early conflicts, or securing an economic future? We all have a private agenda—why must everyone pretend it isn't so?

This doesn't mean people do not love each other; it doesn't mean that they don't anguish over each other; it doesn't mean they aren't joyful about one another. The scheme lies in the hidden agenda of the wedding and its ceremonial coverup. The dream lies in the effort to transcend that. And people do transcend that.

A wedding gives ritualized permission for all those things to happen. Our society, like every society, uses the ritual to conceal the risk, to take the poison out. It is the role of the official wedding photographer to fabricate the experience. Participants are too willing to see only what they have been taught to see, what was preconceived.

The ritual quality of the wedding reduces emotional discomfort. As such, it is peacemaking. Covering the tension between the elements of dreams and schemes is the ritual that blands it out. This ritual is so blind to conflict that it often makes it difficult to find the individual drama. It is always hard to photograph a wedding without being either banal or vicious. The surface offers sentimentality; the jaundiced eye finds proof of a totally dishonest experience.

What makes a wedding so difficult to portray and, at the same time, so incredibly fascinating is that it pulls all that—the pain and the joy, the dreams and the schemes—together. That's what makes it really extraordinary. And weddings do it for ordinary people, for absolutely everybody who gets married.

I believe everyone who gets married is a hero, an awesome superhero. They really are—because they're taking a chance, putting their lives on the line. They're taking a chance that their dreams and their schemes can be brought together. And frankly, yes, the chances are against them on that. And then they have to go to bed with each other—they're right there in their nakedness.

Weddings offer all the diversity of life itself. There are two-minute weddings for a dying parent's last request, or for the Army's permission to live together on the base, or for a tax deduction, or for the approval of a co-op board. There are elaborate "mock" weddings for the elderly, who must have some ritual to legitimize their relationship, but who can not afford the cut in social-security payments that would result from a legal wedding. There are the unofficial ceremonies that unite the lives of two men or of two women. There are stately weddings in cathedrals, and intimate weddings in the woods; weddings are in judges' private chambers during lunch hour, in poor homes with chickens and goats in attendance, in prisons, old age homes, school cafeterias.

In all this variation, what then is common to weddings?

They are never casual. Whether in blue jeans, or formal gown and tuxedo, the bride and groom have decided, in advance, with careful deliberation, what image of themselves they want to live with and to project.

There are never only two people involved. Individuals don't marry. Individuals may live together, but families marry, although the definition of family varies from wedding to wedding. Regardless of their presence or absence on the invitation list, the psychological presence of intimate family members is always felt. And one may marry not only another person, and another family, but another culture as well.

At the extreme, the wedding takes on a life of its own that appears to almost exclude the bride and groom. As one groom told me, "We're just pawns in this great game called a wedding."

Weddings are always unique. Mine were. Yours was, or will be, if you have one. Whether the bridal pair have planned to get married in mid-air in a balloon, or in zebra costumes near a very special secluded lake, or "without a wedding" at City Hall, or at a home wedding wearing something borrowed from a great-grandmother, or by exchanging perfectly plain, solid-gold rings searched for in every jewelry store in town, the wedding is perceived by its main participants as the special expression of unique people. And they are always right.

Weddings are always traditional. At a wedding at the zoo, the bride's sister runs home to get earrings so the bride can wear something borrowed. The woman who catches the bridal bouquet will be the next to be married. To help her on her way, the man who catches the garter will put it as high on her thigh as he can manage.

Sometimes traditions bend and become open to modern interpretation;

sometimes the meanings are forgotten. Once the flag of virginity for brides, white is now usually taken to mean pure of spirit, or to represent tradition itself. Dousing the bridal couple with rice still carries a wish for their fertility, but fertility can now mean having a book published. Custom decrees that the groom must not see the bride until the ceremony. In one comic bedroom dressing scene, where the bride and groom had lived together for five years, it was decided that it was the bridal gown that the groom must not see, so the groom could view the nude bride.

Traditions are the group effort to prevent the unexpected. They help calm the tension. They give us rules that help get us through this day.

Weddings are not sexy for the bride and groom. At the least, this is true right up until they are pronounced husband and wife, when the new legitimacy of sex is indicated in the allowed public kiss. Before that the sexual meaning of this event is seen mainly in its denial.

Even the most flamboyant bride will wear, if not white, a muted shade of beige or blue. Brides with low-cut white gowns will have a thin veil of lace almost to the chin. Grooms wearing a casual shirt meant to be open to the navel, will button it to the neck for this occasion. If allowed to be together before the ceremony, bride and groom seldom touch one another. One does not wish to offend—God, the gods, relatives, the superego? In spite of radical change in sexual rules in the past half-century, there is a sense of what is sexually not "allowed" before marriage that reappears on the wedding day, even for couples who have been sexually intimate for years.

Meanwhile, for their besotted guests, weddings are occasions to roustabout, cast an eye over the available, and generally rejoice in lasciviousness.

There is always tension. Romance and reality collide here. It is different being married. The issue is permanence, of course. The wedding is final. We live in a culture where marriage is based on love, and love is fluid and uncertain. Weddings, in short, have all the promise and romance of security, though everyone old enough to get married is also old enough to know better.

And quite apart from the specter of a failed union that ends in divorce, everyone getting married knows there are unwelcome compromises to come, though they don't yet know the specifics of those compromises.

When I first started to make photographs for this book, it was hard to understand how otherwise rational people could be sweating over the delivery of a pink, rather than a red, corsage. Today I see those "trivial" upsets as a useful cover for the very real reasons for tension. To worry about the "arrangements" is usefully distracting—one need not think "what will my life be like?"

Toothaches, backaches, headaches, hangovers are common. And the couples who have been living together for years are just as tense as the couples who wed after a formal courtship—perhaps more so. And for good reason.

Every wedding has a story. It is most often secret. Sometimes someone tells me at the end of the party, when we are drunk, and I finally understand the specific reasons behind the tension, the crying, the joy I have been photographing all day.

—The groom's father has tried for three years to prevent this marriage. He tried to have his son transferred to another city, arranged camping trips where he and his son would have long hours to talk, ranted and raved, quietly argued his objections. He accepts his failure. He has come, and will offer a toast.

—The elderly bride and groom have both made arrangements to be buried next to their first, departed spouses when they die.

—The two brothers were once very close. They loved the same woman. They still love each other. But they are not so close anymore.

—The groom went off at nine in the morning to get a haircut. His hair was almost to his waist. But he knew that embarrassed his bride in front of her parents. He isn't sure if he'll let it grow again.

—The groom has dated women he loved more, but he is thirty and wants to run for political office next year.

—In between the stop at the photographer's and the reception, the couple will detour for a brief visit to the bride's grandfather, who is dying in a hospital. They hope this afternoon he will not yet be in a coma. The bride was raised by her grandparents until she was fourteen.

—The bride lied. She isn't really pregnant. She'll wait another month, and then tell him she's miscarried.

—The bride has not lied. They know it may not be his baby. They'll know when it's born. They don't know how he'll feel if it isn't his.

They are the stories that make wonderful gossip. And they could make you cry.

>9A   10   ▷—10A   11   —11A   1

>15A   16   ▷—16A   17   ▷—17A   1

>21A   22   ▷—22A   2

I usually arrive several hours before the ceremony. Everyone is already tense. Will the bride remember exactly what she wanted to say at the ceremony, or should she read it? Will the groom remember the ring? What if the bride faints? Everyone is concentrating on makeup, and flowers, and clothes, and cars. Waiting. The anxiety is catching.

As one groom told me, "This doesn't seem real, even though we've been through all the plans and we've been to the chapel before. It just doesn't seem real. Of course, who can imagine what it really means to make this commitment?"

Unbelievable. Can anyone really understand what they are doing? There is free choice, or so we want to believe. In modern times, it is not a matchmaker who decides who will marry whom. Today, almost everyone has to think about it and has to make their own decision.

Our modern couple has spent years finding one another. Some have truly traveled around the world; ironically, they often find the boy or girl next door. But they have done that work. They have been to singles bars, bluffing their sophistication while quaking that they will be rejected because they are too old?, too young?, overweight?, or simply boring? They have developed careers that put them in contact with outstanding members of the opposite sex. They have gone through four years of hated college courses, danced at parties when they wanted to curl up and read, rented summer cottages with people they didn't like, cheered at political rallies to which they were only half committed, all to put themselves in position to meet and attract Mr. or Ms. Right.

On a deeper level, they have gone through five years of psychotherapy, been through bad first marriages, had love affairs with persons already claimed, all to become the persons they are today. They have done the work; and it was not easy.

But they will not deal with that today. The tension is focused on the immediate details, and relieved by a hug, a touched hand, the funny reminiscence of the first meeting. Long, quiet moments to think will not help now.

Of course, nothing really could go wrong. If the musicians don't arrive, forget the music. Likewise the flowers, and the cake. If the ring is lost, a ring can be borrowed. Did the Rabbi's car run out of gas? Have the party today and the ceremony, without the guests, tomorrow. Nothing could really prevent this marriage now.

Unless he changed his mind. Which is so unlikely that there's no point in even thinking about it.

If she wanted to change her mind now, could she? Could you do that? I couldn't.

. . . but the string quartet, or the rock band, or the flautist has arrived, and the right color thread has been found for the attendant's torn hem, and the sister has returned with earrings to borrow, and the Justice of the Peace is downstairs now. The ceremony can get started in just 5 minutes . . .

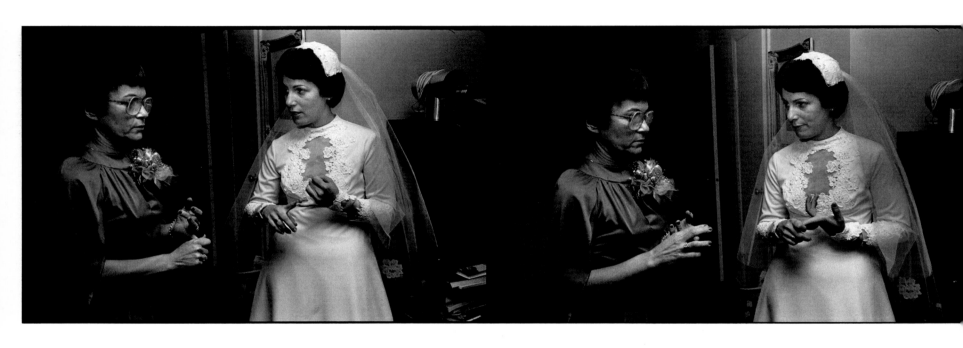

WEDDING DREAMS

I dreamed I was riding up in an elevator and water was pouring in. I was afraid I was going to drown.

My father and Jim were playing tennis together. Jim scored the winning point, and my father jumped over the net to thank him.

We were traveling through the Amazon jungle, and Ginger started complaining that she didn't want to go any farther.

I dreamed about my first lover, Martin. He had stopped coming around and had stopped calling, so I went to see him. It was clear that he was ending the relationship before I wanted to. I kept saying to myself, "That's cool. He has the right to end it whenever he wants. We're both free to do whatever we want." And I was very determined not to be angry. And then we were lying on the ground, making love. And I saw a huge hole in the ground, near some tree roots. And I pushed him in.

I dreamed that my best friend from painting class called our art professor to tell him that I was going to have a very small and intimate show. And he said, "Why's she having a show now? Doesn't she know that all her good work was in the first show, and she'll never make good paintings again?"

I dreamed I couldn't find a suit for the wedding, so I had to come naked.

I was being very aggressive, picking Chris up and carrying him around as though I owned him. But he wasn't a baby, he was a grown man I was carrying around. He was my sexual toy. It made me feel very powerful, and very sexual, and great.

I dreamed a salesman
came to the new house,
and sold me 51% of The
Dream Company.

I dreamed Susan's family and my family were going
deer hunting. They couldn't find us, so they left
without us. My father thought he saw a doe, but he
wasn't sure. He started shooting anyway. A priest
stepped in front of him. And, of course, he stopped
shooting.

I forgot my wedding ring at
my mother's house. The
Minister said we had an-
other 45 minutes before the
ceremony could begin, so I
went back to get the ring.
As I was coming back to
the ceremony, I was going
over a bridge when, sud-
denly, all four tires on my
car went flat. I couldn't
leave it blocking the bridge,
and time was running out.
But no one came to help.

I dreamed I'd decided to
wear my mother's wedding
dress. Tom and I went to
the middle of the floor to
dance. Everyone was
watching us. The dress was
terribly tight; I was strug-
gling to dance with him. I
could hardly move.

I got to the Judge's office a
few minutes before the ceremony. I saw Charlie, in a
black silk dress, chatting
with the Judge. I was
scared. Something was
wrong with his wearing
that dress, but I didn't
know what. "Well, what's
wrong?" he said, looking at
me. I couldn't explain it. It
just made me very anxious.

There was practically no one at the ceremony, except
Beverly and me. The few who were there were
nervous. The poems never got read. It was a 30-second
ceremony. That's all there was, and I was so disap-
pointed. And afterwards, I saw the ring on my hand,
and that was the only thing that had changed.

I dreamed we were all climbing a mountain. Zach was
in the lead, and he was clearing the path. My kids were
between us; I was bringing up the rear. It was a
wonderful dream because I felt the kids were cared for.

Candide: Soon, when we feel we can afford it,
We'll build a modest little farm.

Cunegonde: We'll buy a yacht and live aboard it,
Rolling in luxury and stylish charm.

Cows and chickens.

Social whirls.

Peas and cabbage.

Ropes of pearls.

Soon there'll be little ones beside us,
We'll have a sweet Westphalian home.

Somehow we'll grow as rich as Midas,
We'll live in Paris when we're not in Rome.

Smiling babies.

Marble halls.

Sunday picnics.

Costume balls.

Oh, won't my robes of silk and satin be chic!

I'll have all that I desire.

Pangloss will tutor us in Latin and Greek,
While we sit before the fire.

Glowing rubies.

Glowing logs.

Faithful servants.

Faithful dogs.

We'll round the world enjoying high life;

All will be pink champagne and gold.

We'll lead a rustic and a shy life
Feeding the pigs and sweetly growing old.

Breast of peacock.

Apple pie.

I love marriage.

So do I.

Together: Oh, happy pair!
Oh, happy we!
It's very rare
How we agree.

Together: Oh, happy pair!
Oh, happy we!
It's very rare
How we agree.

The independent bride and groom bow to a higher authority. It may be God, or law, or parents, or community, or tradition. No matter how individualistic we are, we participate in the life of the greater community. The event is larger than ourselves.

The ceremony is a still freeze. Little moves. Much is said, little is heard. There is seldom a joke; when there is, the relief is so great it is met by applause.

The tension lasts right up to the point of pronouncing "husband and wife." It is as though one might change one's mind. This often happens in movies. It never, ever happens in real life. But it *is* a possibility.

The ceremony is replete with symbolism. The bride may be "given away" by her father or, with some feminist consciousness, by both parents. Or she may proclaim, by omitting that part of the traditional ceremony, that she controls her own life and is not available to be "given away" at all.

The commitment may be to love, honor, and obey, or a modern couple may substitute the promise to love and to cherish. They may vow to be man and wife, or to be spouses. They may promise whatever they promise till death do them part, or for as long as it makes them both happy.

But a promise is made in a public arena. And the essence of the ceremony is to create a silent, solemn moment, so that all can hear the commitment to that promise, "I do."

Do you take this person

To be your lawfully wedded spouse

To have and to hold

To love and to cherish

For better
And for worse

For richer
For poorer

In sickness
And in health

From this day forth

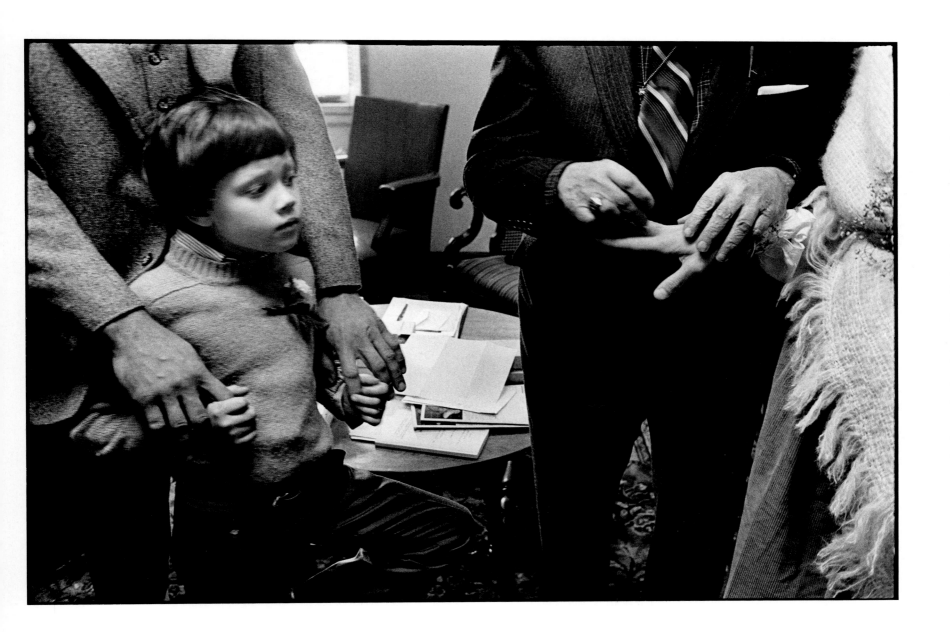

Till death do you part?

The celebration is mostly drunken, even before liquor is served. On the receiving line, men as well as women are allowed to kiss and hug. Children, released from the silence of the 20-minute ceremony, run wild through the church. Questions that seemed all-important in the hours just before the ceremony—whether the ring bearer could stay awake that long, or whether the table flowers would still be fresh in the evening—are now answered, but people never seem to care anymore, one way or the other. The tears and the celebration are for joy, or for sadness, but also for the relief of tension. Something enormous has happened.

The bride and groom will seldom have a moment alone, and may tell me they welcome the departure of the guests, though on occasion they appear to fear that departure as well.

Sexual jokes are suddenly profuse. Shaving cream is brought out to the parking lot to mark the get-away car: "Today she got hers, tonight he'll get his." Or the bride who has been living with her groom for ten years exclaims, "Now we can commit adultery."

Of course, the beginning is here. But endings also start here, for weddings are as much about good-byes as about the new life to come.

The bride's mother, who may have been working on the arrangements for six months, suddenly comes face-to-face with the realization that she has indeed lost a daughter. And she has not gained a son, but rather a son-in-law, which may be quite another thing.

Even if a child adores his new stepmother, he may suddenly realize that she has children of her own, who have a longer and more intimate history with her. And there is also the fear that those children may become closer to his father than he is.

I come to the celebration in a spirit of joy, but it is not a time of simple joy. It is a reflection on all the stuff of life.

By all means marry; if you get a good wife, you'll be happy. If you get a bad one, you'll become a philosopher. *Socrates*

Husbands are like fires—they go out when unattended. *Zsa Zsa Gabor*

There are two kinds of faithfulness in love: one is based on forever finding new things to love in the loved one; the other is based on our anxiety about being faithless. *adapted from La Rochefoucauld*

Love well and fight fair. *Anonymous*

If you are afraid of loneliness, don't marry. *Chekhov*

It destroys one's nerves to be amiable every day to the same human being. *Disraeli*

It doesn't much signify whom one marries, for one is sure to find out the next morning that it was someone else. *Rogers*

Never eat crackers in bed. *Advise from my mother's best friend.*

There are 4,768,000,000 people in the world; and of all those people you have each chosen to marry each other. Don't try to change each other. *Anonymous*

One thing you're going to learn by being married is how different people are. *Peggy Papp*

One morning you're going to wake up and look at each other and wonder why in the world you ever married each other. Don't panic. *Advise from a wedding sermon by Algernon Black*

Marriage is a romance in which the hero dies in the first chapter.
Anonymous

A man has no business to marry a woman who can't make him miserable. It means she can't make him happy.   *G. B. Shaw*

The best part of marriage is the fights—the rest is merely so-so.   *Thornton Wilder*

The critical period in matrimony is breakfast time.   *A. P. Herbert*

It is not good that the man should be alone.   *Genesis II. 18*

Two octopuses got married and walked down the isle arm in arm in arm in arm in arm in arm . . .
from the film Irreconcilable Differences

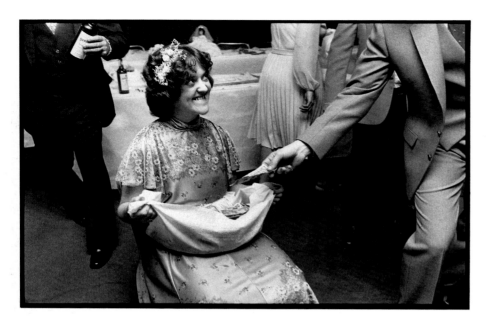

"More and better sex," the maid of honor toasts.
"With Jeffrey," says the groom's sister.

"Of course, I'm delighted," the bride's former room-
mate tells me. "But you've got to realize that I've
always been her best friend until now, and the fact is
I'm definitely in second place now."

The bride tells me, "The arrangements seemed so gaudy and pretentious. I kept
telling him, 'Tom, if you really love me, we'll elope.'"

The teenage daughter of the groom starts a toast,
"When my brother and I first met Joanne, we didn't
like her one bit."

The best man tells me, "Listen, I love him, and if he
weren't my best friend, I wouldn't be here. It's tough
coming to a wedding when you're going through a
divorce."

"I'd just about given up
on you," said the groom's
mother.

A guest tells me her daughter is getting married soon.
"I tried to talk her out of it," she says.
"Why?" I ask.
"I couldn't understand why anyone would want to be married." she says.
"Why?" I ask.
"Excuse me," she said and left to get a drink.

"I don't love him," the bride admits to me. "But I think he's wonderful. And all the men I loved were terrible."

"I'm so happy to be marrying Gayle," the groom tells me, "Because she's so happy. I come home every night and she acts like she just won the lottery."

The mother of the groom, who has missed the ceremony to finish the preparations of food for the feast for 300 people, explains to me, "That's what family is for."

"You've done well. Congratulations," said the bride's uncle.

To me, the bride and the groom seemed to have nothing in common. The best man toasts them, "To their ability to build love out of diversity."

"I wish you all the happiness you can stand," a guest tells the groom.

"Just keep doing whatever it is that you're doing," the bride's mother tells her.

A bride tells me, "I just pray this doesn't change anything for us."

The photographs on pages 20, 49, and 68–69 were taken before and during a 2,000-couple mass wedding of the Universalist ("Moonie") Church, at Madison Square Garden in New York City, in 1982. The photographs on pages 53, 54, and 55 were all taken at the Office of Civil Marriage Commissioners, in Las Vegas, Nevada, in 1983. The photograph on page 61 was taken at a wedding chapel in Las Vegas, Nevada in 1983. The photograph on page 37 is of a bride saying confession on the morning of her wedding day, in Merida, Yucatan, 1980. All of the photographs in this book were taken in the United States or Mexico from 1979 through 1986, at events and places that were part of a wedding day.